Brigitte Weninger was born in Kufstein, Austria, and spent twenty years working as a kindergarten teacher before trying her hand at writing. She has since published more than fifty books, which have been translated into thirty languages worldwide. She continues to be heavily involved in promoting literacy and storytelling.

Julie Wintz-Litty has been an illustrator since 1994. Her career began while working with Michael Neugebauer at Nord-Sud. From there she worked as a graphic designer and painter. While not illustrating, she attends book fairs and teaches art workshops.

First published in the United States, Great Britain, Canada, Australia, and New Zealand in 2018 by NorthSouth Books, Inc., an imprint of NordSüd Verlag AG, CH-8050 Zürich, Switzerland.

Distributed in the United States by NorthSouth Books, Inc., New York 10016.
Library of Congress Cataloging-in-Publication Data is available.
ISBN: 978-0-7358-4326-4 (trade edition)
3 5 7 9 11 • 10 8 6 4
Printed in China, 2022
www.northsouth.com

MIX
Paper | Supporting responsible forestry
FSC
www.fsc.org
FSC® C144853

Silent Night

The wonderful story
of the beloved Christmas carol

Brigitte Weninger
Julie Wintz-Litty

North
South

$\mathcal{E}$veryone has experienced the joys of silent, holy nights—when a longed-for child is born, a difficult period of life is finally over, or we suddenly realize that all things are connected.

This book tells of such experiences, and of how a beautiful song first came into the world.

On the crisp, cold Christmas Eve of 1818, in the Austrian village of Oberndorf, a young priest named Josef Mohr opened his door and saw his student Lucas trudging across the churchyard. The boy was carrying his little sister Lisa on his back. She had been ill for a long time and could no longer walk unaided.

"Good morning, Father!" cried the children. "Please may we go to the church with you?"

"Hello to the two of you!" said Mohr cheerfully. "Of course you can come to the rehearsal. Lucas can help at the organ. But we should wait by the warm stove until Mr. Gruber arrives. Come in."

The priest took the children into his study, gave each of them a piece of bread, and asked, "How are your parents and your brothers and sisters?"

"Better," said Lucas. "Our father got a job as a courier. And Grandma is living with us now, and helps us to get enough to eat. She knows about so many herbs and spices! Some of them even grow under the snow."

"Do you know why food is so scarce this year?" Lisa asked the priest. "The neighbors say this famine is a punishment from God."

"Nonsense!" said the priest. "There are very different reasons. Look. . . ."

Father Mohr took a large atlas from the bookshelf. He showed them a map of the world and said, "Three years ago, a volcano named Tambora erupted on this Pacific island, far away from here. It threw huge amounts of ash up in the air. It was a natural disaster that killed thousands of people. And now these clouds of ash are traveling around the earth so that the sunshine can't get through. That's why . . ."

"That's why it's cold everywhere and the plants can't grow," said Lucas thoughtfully. "When plants are sick, humans and animals have nothing to eat. And because it's raining and snowing so much, there are floods. And because of the floods and the ice floes in the river, our father and the other boatmen can't travel. And if people can't do their jobs, they have no money to buy bread. It's all connected!"

"Exactly," said the priest. "You're a clever boy."

Suddenly, there was a knock at the door.

"That must be Mr. Gruber," cried Lucas, rushing out of the study. He really liked the teacher, who came from the nearby village of Arnsdorf. He was everybody's friend, was a wonderful organist and guitarist, and also had a lovely singing voice.

"Good morning, teacher!" cried Lucas happily.

"Ah, you already have visitors," Franz Xaver Gruber said laughingly to the priest.

He shook both children by the hand then gave his friend Josef a cheerful slap on the shoulder.

"Shall we go into the church and rehearse? With all this misery around us, we can at least have a Merry Christmas mass. Come on, Lisa, I'll give you a piggyback ride."

Together they all entered the cold, damp, but brightly decorated Church of St. Nicholas. After the town of Laufen had been divided, this was the new parish church of Oberndorf.

"Brrr, it's cold in here!" said Gruber
with a shiver as he went up to the
organ loft with Lucas and Lisa. There
he sat down at the organ and asked,
"Is my assistant ready?"

"Yes, teacher," said Lucas.
Then with all his might he pumped the leather bellows that
drove air into the pipes of the organ. Gruber pulled out the stops
and started to play, but instead of a beautiful melody, what came
out were all sorts of horrible screechy noises.

Mohr was shocked and went rushing up to the organ loft.

"That sounds awful!" said Lisa.

"Maybe it's because of the cold," suggested Lucas. "Can't you tune the organ—like a guitar?"

"No, this is going to take a long time to repair, and it'll cost a lot of money," said Gruber. "But the Midnight Mass is tonight, and the villagers are looking forward to it."

They all looked helplessly at one another.

"Let's sing something," suggested Lisa.

"We sing at every mass," said Mohr despairingly.

"Then what we need is a special song," said Gruber. "Not just a hymn but a beautiful, festive Christmas song."

"Can you compose such a Christmas song?" asked Lucas hopefully.

"No," replied Gruber. "First you need a beautiful text or a poem. Then you compose a melody that will go with it."

"Um . . . I might have a poem for you," said Mohr rather timidly. "It's actually about the holy night."

"Let's see it, Josef!" cried Gruber.

Mohr hurried away and returned a few minutes later with a sheet of paper. He stood beside the altar and read the following poem out to the empty church:

"Silent night, holy night,
All is calm, all is bright
Round yon virgin mother and child.
Holy infant, so tender and mild,
Sleep in heavenly peace,
Sleep in heavenly peace."

"That sounds really lovely!" Gruber said excitedly, "and I can already hear a little melody. But I need an instrument to compose with. . . . Josef, may I borrow your guitar?"

"Of course," said Mohr. "It's just been restrung and tuned. Come on, let's go back to the house."

Lucas and Lisa sat motionless on the bench and watched their teacher at work. Sometimes Gruber would hum or mumble to himself, but then he would pluck the strings again and draw black signs on the lined paper.

"What's he doing now?" whispered Lisa.

"He's writing musical notes," her brother explained. "They're like letters. If you understand the notes, you know exactly what to play or sing. I'm learning that too."

Gruber smiled at Lucas and went on writing. *"Si–i–lent night, ho–o–ly night . . ."*

At midday, the teacher put down his pen and cried, "Done! Lucas, fetch Father Mohr. Then go and find the choirmaster and tell him the choir must come straightaway to the church for a rehearsal."

"I'm on my way, teacher!" said Lucas, his face beaming, and away he ran.

Gruber picked up another sheet of music paper and began to write the song down for the church choir.

It was very late by the time everything was ready.
And then the Midnight Mass began.

Many of the congregation wore the same shabby
clothes they had worn during the day. In this terrible
winter of famine, people could not afford to buy new
things. Instead of a festive meal, most families had
nothing to eat but a slice of bread and jam.

And so they all crowded into the Church of St. Nicholas, the young and the old, hoping to find some comfort in their togetherness.

But there was an extra excitement in the atmosphere this Christmas—a buzz of curiosity. Some of the congregation had heard that the young priest and the teacher had prepared something special.

The mass proceeded as usual, though, except that there was no organ.

Then came the moment that Lucas and Lisa had been waiting for.

Franz Xaver Gruber walked slowly to the front and stood by the altar with a single sheet of music in his hand. Father Josef Mohr picked up his guitar.

The church fell silent in hushed expectation. Then the two friends began to sing:

"Silent night, holy night . . ."

The beautiful melody filled the church, and everyone listened, entranced.

When the choir repeated the first verse, Lucas and Lisa joined in with their high, clear voices. And then the whole congregation sang:

"Silent night, holy night . . ."

After the mass, people shook hands and wished one another a happy and peaceful Christmas. There was a rare feeling of comfort and goodwill as they made their way home that evening, and many had tears of joy in their eyes.

They had been deeply moved, and they knew that they really had experienced something special. It had lit a spark of hope that warmed their hearts.

But that is not the end of the song's story. On the contrary, it's just the beginning.

About a year later, the organ builder Carl Mauracher came to Oberndorf from the Tyrol to repair the organ.

When he heard the carol for the first time, he loved it. "It's beautiful!" he cried. "Would you mind if I made a copy of it?"

Gruber did not mind at all.

And so the organ builder took the score back to his home, and that Christmas he performed it at the Midnight Mass. Among the choir were two families of folk singers, the Rainers and the Strassers. Once again the words and melody of "Silent Night" conquered all hearts.

The Napoleonic wars and the years without a summer had also caused great suffering in the Tyrol. The people had barely enough to eat, and some of them scraped out a living by carving household utensils, wooden Christmas scenes, and other objects, and traveling around to sell them.

The Rainers and Strassers were among these families, and they journeyed far to the north.

People there would listen eagerly when the Tyrolean parents and children sang in the marketplace about their beautiful home in the mountains, but the song that touched their hearts most deeply was "Silent Night."

Even the newspapers carried reports.

In 1833 the carol was published for the first time. Now its fame spread even more rapidly.

The two musical families, in their colorful Tyrolean costumes, were invited to many different places. They sang to kings and princes, performed in imperial palaces, and even went as far as America.

Many migrants also took the song with them, and they would sing it at Christmas in their new homes on the other side of the world.

It was sung in schools and churches, in community centers, on ships, and even in the trenches of both sides during the two world wars.

People in foreign lands who heard the song in German wanted to sing it in their own language.

To date it has been translated into more than three hundred different languages— and the list is still growing! It is like a river of words and music, getting greater and mightier as it flows through the world.

And so from its small beginnings in a tiny Austrian village, "Silent Night" has made its way all around the planet, reaching even as far as you. Because you too can sing:

"Silent night, holy night,
All is calm, all is bright . . ."

Josef Mohr

Josef Mohr was born in Salzburg, Austria, in 1792. He came from a very poor home, but one of his teachers recognized the boy's talent and helped him to get a proper education so that eventually he could become a priest and a musician. He wrote the poem "Silent Night" in 1816, and the following year he was sent to the Church of St. Nicholas in Oberndorf, where he became friends with Franz Xaver Gruber. The two of them gave the song its first performance in 1818.

In 1819 Mohr was transferred to a neighboring parish. He died in Wagrain in 1848.

Josef Mohr was never painted or photographed during his life. Long after he died, the Austrian priest and sculptor Josef Mühlbacher had Mohr's skull exhumed, and ever since then this has been the model used for statues and paintings of him.

(Conrad) Franz Xaver Gruber

Franz Xaver Gruber was born in the Austrian village of
Hochburg-Ach in 1787. He was expected to become a linen
weaver like his father, but a teacher recognized his musical
gifts and enabled him to get the appropriate education.
Gruber taught at the school in Arnsdorf, but at the same time
he was the organist and sexton at the church in neighboring
Oberndorf. He was married three times and fathered fourteen
children, though sadly only four of them survived into
adulthood. Times were very hard in those days. He died in
Hallein in 1863, a much loved and respected man.

Lucas and Lisa

Lucas and Lisa represent every boy and girl in the world who has had to suffer hunger, disease, and poverty. And yet many such children view the future with hope. They have their dreams and they make their plans. But they need adults by their side to support them. Without the clear-sightedness of their teachers, Mohr and Gruber would never have been able to write their poems or compose their music. And then they in turn did a great deal of good, helping their own students. Help a child and you help the world.

Laufen-Oberndorf

This was a prosperous town in the Archbishopric of Salzburg. Here the Salzach River formed a dangerous bend that only local pilots and ships could navigate. All goods had to be unloaded and then reloaded onto other ships. In 1816, after the end of the Napoleonic wars, the town was divided. Laufen then belonged to Bavaria, Germany, while Oberndorf remained Austrian. Many people lost their jobs. Oberndorf itself was frequently flooded, and the Church of St. Nicholas had to be demolished in 1913.

Silent Night

translated into English
by John Freeman Young in 1859:

Silent night, holy night,
All is calm, all is bright
Round yon virgin mother and child.
Holy infant, so tender and mild,
Sleep in heavenly peace,
Sleep in heavenly peace.

Silent night, holy night,
Shepherds quake at the sight;
Glories stream from heaven afar,
Heavenly hosts sing Alleluia!
Christ the Savior is born,
Christ the Savior is born!

Silent night, holy night,
Son of God love's pure light;
Radiant beams from thy holy face
With the dawn of redeeming grace,
Jesus, Lord, at thy birth,
Jesus, Lord, at thy birth.